Introducing Quakers

by George H. Gorman

QUAKER HOME SERVICE · LONDON

Since *Introducing Quakers* was first published in 1969 it has been the most sought after first introduction to Quaker belief and practice; over 100,000 copies being printed. George Gorman completed his last revision of the book shortly before he died early in 1982. *Introducing Quakers* has continued to be greatly used and Quaker Home Service have felt it right to publish a further reprint, unaltered, to meet this demand.

ISBN 0 85245 005 2

First published May 1969
reprinted May 1970, August 1971 and June 1986
Revised reprints January 1974, March 1978 and September 1981

Friends House Euston Road London NW1 2BJ

Printed in Great Britain by
Newnorth-Burt Ltd College St Kempston Bedford
Cover design and layout by John Blamires

Preface

This short book is intended to introduce Quakers to people who, while they know little about them, are interested to know more. While it is my personal description of what Quakers believe and do, I have tried to make it as objective as possible. With this in mind the original draft was read by some twenty Friends and a few non-Friends. Many more Friends have been involved in subsequent revisions of the text. I gladly acknowledge my debt to them for their criticisms and help, and wherever possible have tried to meet their points and adopt their suggestions. I have deliberately limited myself to the experience of Quakers in Britain and have not attempted to write about Friends in other parts of the world.

Contents

INTRODUCTION

The popular image of Quakers tends to be a confused one. Sometimes they are associated with the manufacture of porridge, at others with a group of rigid puritans holding extremely negative attitudes. Generally Quakers are thought to be 'good' so good in fact that they are quite impossible to live with. Many people persist in thinking of Quakers as wealthy philanthropists: others associate them with reforming movements but regretfully imagine that they became extinct with the death of Elizabeth Fry.

In fact Quakers are very much alive today, and far from being a staid and starchy group, are friendly, warm people with a positive attitude to life. This will, I hope, become obvious in this short book, as my aim in writing is to try to describe the kind of things Quakers believe, what they do and the sort of people they are. I have chosen to write in a personal way, partly because I find it difficult to deal with my subject in a detached impersonal manner, and partly because there is not, and never can be, an official Quaker spokesman. For about thirty years I have been secretary of a committee, one of whose main jobs is to make the existence of Quakers known, and also to assure people, who feel in sympathy with Quaker beliefs and aims, that they would be warmly welcomed to become Quakers themselves.

So although this book is a personal interpretation of Quakerism, it is written from the background of a reasonable knowledge of Quakers themselves, and of people who are interested in them. I have tried to be objective in my presentation, and to indicate as fairly as I can the rich variety of experience to be found among modern Quakers. I shall only make occasional references to history when it is absolutely necessary, or where some incident from the past usefully illustrates an aspect of present day Quaker life.

In order to avoid confusion something must be said at this point about the name 'Quaker'. It is in fact a nickname given to the followers of George Fox in the mid-seventeenth century. Like most nicknames it has stuck fast, so that 300 years later it is by this name that Quakers are best known today. Their official title is 'The Religious Society of Friends', and individual members are usually referred to collectively as Friends or Quakers. In the following pages these names will be used interchangeably as happens in the Society today.

Origins

The first Friends got their nickname partly because some of them did actually quake in their meetings, and partly because of a joke made by a Judge before whom George Fox appeared in 1650 on a charge of blasphemy. Fox told the Judge that he should 'tremble at the word of the Lord', and judicial wit, as sharp then as now, dubbed Fox and his followers 'Quakers'.

It may seem strange that George Fox, who is now widely recognised as a religious genius, should have been arraigned on such a charge. A brief glance at his background will explain the position. Fox was born in the Leicestershire village of Fenny Drayton in 1624; his father Christopher Fox, was known to the villagers as 'righteous Christer' because of his integrity. His mother, Fox says, 'came of the stock of martyrs', for her forebears had been persecuted for their beliefs.

Despite this orthodox environment, Fox himself gradually moved towards a religious outlook that was felt to threaten the patterns of belief widely held by his contemporaries. To Fox these seemed to be largely notional, consisting of theories and speculations that tended to frustrate the development of a truly spiritual life. In nationwide travels, later to be extended to Europe and America, Fox fearlessly proclaimed his understanding that authentic religion was not primarily concerned with accepted religious observances enshrined in church order and dogma, but with a living response to an awareness of spiritual values to be discovered deep in the human personality.

Fox's views were considered heretical and dangerous by the religious establishment, to the point where it resisted them, not only by argument, but also by persecution. There were, however, many people who had been seeking religious freedom and a more spiritual interpretation of their Christian beliefs. Such people warmly welcomed Fox's teaching, so that he quickly found an enthusiastic following among those, who like himself, felt the orthodox religion of the time to be a strait-jacket, rather than a dynamic basis for living.

Christianity was taken with great seriousness in seventeenth century England, but this did not prevent Fox and the early Friends from criticising their fellow Christians, somewhat uncharitably, as 'apostate'. For Friends, being a Christian was not a matter of conformity to doctrine and the observance of forms, but an overwhelming sense of the nearness of God to them through the indwelling spirit of Christ. They felt that they had rediscovered primitive Christianity, and proclaimed that 'Christ had come to teach his people himself'. They were convinced that they could have direct communion with God without the mediation of church or priests, for they relied on the inward authority of the spirit rather than on the outward authority of the church and tradition. While they knew and loved the Bible, they tried to get behind the written word to the sources of its inspiration.

In seeking to describe their experience the metaphor 'light' was constantly on their lips, for it seemed to them that, as William Penn, quoting the New Testament put it, they had come 'out of darkness into God's marvellous light'. In fact, throughout Quaker history phrases such as 'the inward light of Christ' and the less elegant 'inner light', have frequently been used by Quakers in speaking of their deepest experiences.

To sum up this brief description of the convictions of the first Friends I quote again from William Penn. He wrote, 'It is not opinion, or speculation, or notions of what is true, or assent to, or the subscription of articles or propositions, though never so soundly worded, that...makes a man a true believer or a true Christian; but it is a conformity of mind and practice to the will of God, in all holiness of conversation, according to the dictates of this Divine principle of light and life in the soul, which denotes a person truly a child of God.'*

In modern terms we can say that for Fox and his followers the quest for truth started with the awareness of values known in their personal experience, which could rightly be described as spiritual. These were not magical, supernatural qualities injected into them, but the very values that made them truly human. Yet while really their own, these values seemed to have a transcendent quality about them that pointed to a source beyond human life, yet never divorced from it. So the early Quakers could only make sense of life by interpreting it from a religious standpoint; for them religion was not a cold, academic exercise, but the total involvement of themselves in a way of life. They placed their emphasis on an immediate awareness of God in the depths of their inner life, rather than on the concept of a God 'up there' or 'out there'. In the words of Rufus Jones, 'religion. they believed, does not rise outside and flow in; it springs up inside and flows out'.†

In the judgement of the historian G. M. Trevelyan, not himself a Quaker: 'The finer essence of George Fox's queer teaching, common to the excited revivalists who were his first disciples, and to the 'quiet' Friends of later times, was surely this—that Christian qualities matter much more than Christian dogmas. No Church or sect had ever made that its living rule

---

* Quoted in *The Second Period of Quakerism* by W. C. Braithwaite. Second edition ed. by Henry J. Cadbury. Cambridge: Univ. Press, 1961, p.379.

† Jones (Rufus M.) *The Faith and Practice of the Quakers*. London: Methuen 1927, pp. 39-40.

before. To maintain the Christian quality in the world of business and of domestic life, and to maintain it without pretension or hypocrisy, was the great achievement of these extraordinary people. England may well be proud of having produced and perpetuated them. The Puritan pot had boiled over, with much heat and fury; when it had cooled and been poured away, this precious sediment was left at the bottom.'*

Much more could, of course, be said about the religious convictions of the early Friends, and of their understanding of Christianity. I have made this excursion into the past, partly to show, in the briefest possible way, how the Society originated in history, and also to indicate the attitude of the first Quakers to religious faith. Their conviction that the approach to a religious view of life must always begin with ordinary human experience, and that religion essentially demands the total involvement of the human personality, has coloured the whole of Quaker history. These convictions are still powerfully present in modern Quakerism.

Quakers have always been essentially practical in their approach to religion. Their corporate conviction that there is that of God in every one has been the continuing basis of their deep concern for peace and social justice; their interest in prisoners; the proper care of the mentally sick, and their concern for oppressed people everywhere.

Quakers unitedly affirm that life is good: that it has meaning and purpose. They are sustained in this faith by the experience of their meetings for worship where they know these truths experimentally.

---

* Trevelyan (G. M.) *English Social History*. London: Longmans, 1944, p. 267.

1

APPROACH TO FAITH

Something needs to be said at this point about 'faith'. So many people tend to think of faith as an almost magic quality that some have and others do not. In popular use 'faith' is also confused with a system of belief that a believer is required to accept, and far too many people still tend to define faith as the schoolboy did when he said it was 'believing something you know not to be true'.

I want to use the word in the way in which it is widely used by Quakers, who, when they speak of faith generally mean having trust in a person or in an experience. This is not magic or superstition, but an attitude that is open to every one.

Human experience: the point of departure

For Quakers of the late twentieth century, as much as for their predecessors in the seventeenth, the point of departure for their religious quest is, in the first place, their own real, deep human experience. But what is this experience? Most of the time we go about the business of living without thinking consciously about it. From time to time, however, something happens for good or ill, which causes us to think and to meditate profoundly about our very existence. Then we are driven into the depths of our being, where we are vividly aware of ourselves as unique and individual persons.

We struggle to find words to describe that of which we are aware, and they evade us, because no words are fully adequate to express a state that defies definition. Perhaps the words 'life', 'spirit' and 'consciousness' are among those that come most readily to our aid, but even they fail to disclose the full sense of our identity as living beings. Our first reaction to our interior journey may well be one of anxiety, or even of terror, as we sense our insignificance, finitude and loneliness. But as we allow ourselves to be calmed by the stillness at the centre of our being, we can find a deeper awarness of our rootedness in life itself, and of our relatedness to other people. We know that it is from this deep place that our insights in the real meaning of life arise, and that the power to live it is found. In this kind of dynamic, vital experience we realise that we have discovered a new level of existence, in which our spirit is fused with spirit itself in a creative encounter. Religious people of all ages have spoken of this experience as an encounter with God.

Friends have always been cautious about using the name of God too easily, and today many are more acutely aware of this hesitation for a number of reasons. One of their main difficulties is that the word 'God' has often been identified with misleading and false ideas, many of them highly coloured with superstition. A further difficulty is that the word 'God' is frequently used as a kind of intellectual concept, whereas for Quakers their awareness of God is discovered in response and commitment to the deep meaning of life. Quakers also hesitate to use the word too freely because, while completely convinced that people everywhere can know this experience in the depth of their being, they also realise that the ways in which this experience is discovered and expressed by people will vary greatly. The attempt to press this living reponse into a word or words is liable to limit and distort it. This becomes obvious when we consider how inadequate words are to express and define any profound human experience. When a man says to a woman 'I love you', we recognise that the words themselves are quite unable to convey the full power and depth intended. But despite all these legitimate hesitations, and the impossibility of knowing exactly what the word God means, there is in the end no other word in human language that can finally convey the awareness of an encounter that confronts people at the centre of their being.

Personal relationships

In writing of this experience of encounter at the most profound level of our existence I have already said that we are not only vividly aware of our individuality, but also of our relationship and involvement with others. Undoubtedly, the experience of loving relationships provides for many Friends one of the clearest insights into the real nature of life and its meaning. Furthermore, the language we use naturally to describe such relationships lends itself most readily to our attempts to describe our awareness of the spiritual qualities of life.

It is widely recognised nowadays that there is a deep human need for people to be able to love and to be loved. If children are to develop into mature adults it is necessary for them to receive affection, sympathy, understanding and security, and be made to feel wanted and significant. They must also be able to express their innate capacity for love by loving the people among whom they live. If their environment is such that it frustrates their need to develop such a normal human relationship, they are described as 'deprived' children, and it is recognised that it will be more difficult for them to grow into mature persons. The human need to experience loving relationships does not cease with the achievement of adulthood. Throughout life people, if they are to be real mature persons, must continue to develop and maintain adequate relationships with others. While not ignoring the fact that the human capacity to give and to receive love varies tremendously, there is no doubt that if it is in any way unsatisfied, there is a strong likelihood of the development of a personality that is stunted or warped. In all this it is important not to confuse loving and liking. We often dislike various things about people, but this does not make it impossible to have a loving attitude towards them, although it may make it more difficult to achieve.

The recognition of the overwhelming importance of the power of love for the adequate development of the mature human person could be accepted as an insight gained through psychological knowledge. For Quakers it is also a profound religious insight discovered in and through ordinary human experience. The name 'Society of Friends' is no accident; in seeking to respond to life in an attitude of love Friends, as a community of people, find a sense of meaning and purpose that leads to authentic living. For it is one way of looking at the world, which, while it does not claim to explain everything about it, nevertheless is of ultimate importance in providing a vital clue to the nature of human life, and to the way in which it should be lived.

It is very easy when reflecting upon the importance of human love to be sentimental about it and to overlook the fact that courage, strength and tenacity are as much its ingredients as gentle tenderness. It is also easy to forget that for many people the experience of loving relationships is the exception rather than the rule. I have just said that for Quakers the recognition of the power of love in human life is a religious as well as a psychological insight. To this religious insight they are convinced Jesus made an outstanding (some would say unique) contribution, by his life and teaching, and by the way in which he met his death. People who look into the depths of their being and find only terror, confusion, hatred and bitterness, which convinces them that life has no meaning or loving purpose, may well find that the experience of Jesus can bring new hope. A similar hope may well come to isolated or lonely people who have through the circumstances of their lives found it difficult to achieve loving relationships.

Quakerism began when George Fox made his lonely search for something in which his life could find meaning and purpose. The advice of his relatives, his doctor and his friends was of little help to him, and consultations with Christian ministers failed to satisfy him. It was at this point of near despair that, as he records in his Journal, he heard an inner voice which said, ' "There is one even Christ Jesus who can speak to thy condition", and when I heard it my heart did leap for joy.' The sense of joyful release that Fox discovered has been echoed down the three centuries of Quaker history until the present, and fortifies Friends in their conviction that anyone can find new understanding because of the trust in and response to life made by Jesus, and exemplified by the manner of his living.

The Book of Christian Discipline (see p. 27 where I describe it) witnesses to the experience of countless Friends who for more than 300 years, speak of God as caring for, loving and sustaining them. Quite simply they know God.

What I have written in no way contradicts or denies the validity of this experience. But for many people today the use of such 'God-language' is an insurmountable barrier because it does not seem to relate to their feelings and thoughts of how things are. I think I know a little of the way they feel because although I was brought up in a strong and devout Christian atmosphere I found much of the traditional religious language becoming irrelevant. So I had to re-think the truths it was trying to express.

In writing this chapter, and others to follow, I have tried to help my readers to see how Quakers in the past and present look at the ordinary things of life and rightly interpret them as providing what traditionally have been held to be experiences of God.

2

QUAKERS AND CHRISTIANITY

Quakers and Jesus

I hope I shall make it clear in what I write that the Society of Friends encourages, and is enriched by, the variety of approach to religious faith made by its members. It is important to note this feature of the Society at this point when I am about to describe the attitude of Friends to the central figure of Christianity. The Society has never required its members to conform to a particular view about Jesus, holding that the only valid test of Christians is whether they live in the spirit of Christlike love, and not what they say they believe. In such an atmosphere of freedom it is natural for there to be a great range of views about the place Jesus occupies in modern Quaker thought. In trying to interpret this aspect of Quakerism I am inevitably biased in the direction of my own convictions, but nevertheless I hope what I write is a fair indication of the range of views I know to exist in the Society.

There is no doubt in my mind that Friends generally accept as a fact of history that Jesus was an outstandingly great religious teacher, steeped in the rich religious tradition of the Jewish people. Friends would also accept that Jesus interpreted this tradition in an astonishingly new manner, adding to it by his insight, thought and life a fresh and creative approach to religious awareness; the validity of his contribution being shown by its continuing impact on the minds of men. Most Friends would agree further that the essence of the teaching of Jesus is to be found in his insistence that people should love God with all their being, and should love their neighbours as themselves. To achieve these attitudes they need a radical change of outlook.

What I have written so far, is, I think, a fair assessment of Friends' wide acceptance of Jesus as a profound religious teacher and giant among the prophets. For them Jesus penetrated deeply into the meaning of life, and saw love at its centre. To this love he responded in personal trust as the ultimate source and sustenance of life itself. For Jesus, God must at least be like this. By his absolute trust in this love, and by the way it influenced his life and enabled him to accept his death, Jesus made it actual in his personality—he lived it into being. So in him we have a window into God, for in his life the love that is God is most clearly seen. Thus Jesus discloses God to men.

In writing in this way about Jesus we must not distort the fact that he was a man, born of human parents. He undoubtedly made a tremendous impact on many people, some of whom found relief from physical illness as a result of their trust in him. In their desire to emphasise his supreme value to them, some of his followers in later years described his life and activities in miraculous terms. Whether we accept this explanation is not important; what matters is the greatness of his personality and his spiritual insight. Because his teaching and way of life ran counter to the convictions and practices of the religious leaders of his time, they, with the consent of the populace, engineered his trial and execution. Men do not like goodness if it challenges their moral failure, or loyalty to truth that calls for a revolutionary change of mind. They killed Jesus because they were afraid of him.

As in his life, so in his approach to death Jesus never faltered in his trust in love, and forgave those who rejected him. By this creative attitude Jesus radically changed a most heinous act of human wickedness into an event that has released love and forgiveness into a dark world. For ever after people know that such love can overcome evil, and in this knowledge have found freedom to live.

Many Friends are sceptical about the New Testament accounts of the physical resurrection of Jesus, although for some this is a crucial element in their faith. Most would agree that the essential meaning behind the story of the first Easter is that death could not destroy all that was of real value in the earthly life of Jesus. The love experienced by his disciples could not be taken from them by his death, because they recognised that it was of an infinite and eternal quality. In fact, it was only after his death that they came to understand and to appreciate fully the deep meaning of his life and to be set free by it.

This view will not, I am sure, satisfy those Friends, who see in Jesus a unique revelation of the living God in history, who after his death was resurrected by the power of God's spirit, and continues to live as the eternal Christ, with whose spirit his followers may enter into a living communion. Nor will what I have written commend itself to those Friends for whom Jesus is no more than one among the world's religious leaders and prophets. But I believe that I have fairly described something of the attitude of the considerable group of Friends whose convictions lie between these two positions.

Quakers and religious experience

It is now necessary to make it clear that while the experience of personal relationships provides an extremely valuable insight into the meaning and purpose of life, it is by no means the only source of religious awareness. At the still centre of their lives many Friends realise the oneness with all created things and a sense of identity with the spirit of God the lifegiver. 'That of God in everyone' is a well-loved Quaker phrase. This awareness leads some Friends to speak of an experience of direct communion with God and of immediate guidance in the affairs of daily life. The degree of what may be called 'mystical awareness' varies greatly among Friends. In some it is practically non-existent, in others it is the most potent influence in their lives. For many it is centred in the experience of the indwelling Christ. For others it is focused in and enriched by their love of nature. Great art, music and literature provide, for a large number of Quakers, rich sources of religious inspiration. The breadth of their understanding of the nature of religious experience, and the variety of its expression among them, has led Quakers to a wide tolerance of other religions, and a deep respect for the truths they enshrine.

It is impossible to write about religious experience without saying something about prayer and the way in which the life of the spirit is sustained. Prayer is such a personal activity that I can only write about it from my own experience. Although I was brought up to 'say my prayers' and, in fact, to pray about anything, I ceased to pray in a formal, orthodox way a long time ago. The change came so gradually that I only noticed it when I found it difficult to use particular prayers, and later to try to speak to God as I had been taught.

I do not recall feeling any sense of loss about this change in my attitude to prayer, nor do I remember feeling too guilty about it. I know many Friends who are able to engage in a kind of dialogue with God, and who are sustained by a sense of spiritual presence in their regular quiet times. While I respect their sincerity, and recognise the validity of their experience, I have come to realise that this way is not for me.

This does not mean that I have lost all awareness of the experience that Christians normally describe by the word 'prayer'. This was brought home to me some years ago when my wife and I spent some time with a friend who was facing a crisis in her life. We felt that we were most inadequate in the help and comfort we were able to offer to her. But after she had left us we found we were in some strange way, continuing to wrestle with her problem as if it were our own. We began to see life through her eyes and, to this extent, were sharing her burden, so that she was no longer alone with it. We knew we had experienced part of what people mean when they say they are praying for someone.

Such an involvement with people would be a mere escape unless we immediately try to see how it is possible to answer the kind of prayer we would have prayed for them. There may be nothing we can actually do for the particular person concerned, but the effort to love and to uphold them can open our eyes to the possibility of caring, in some practical way, for someone encountered in our daily life. Certainly it should help to make us more sensitive to the people around us.

Even when we are sensitively aware of people's needs, we often lack the energy to act because of our inability to overcome our selfish lethargy. Here, the more orthodox Christian would say, is where the love and power of God operate, and I would not want to deny this. My difficulty is in speaking in this way for the reasons mentioned earlier.

However, I do know that trying to be open to things that are good, and beautiful, and true, wherever they are to be found, brings to me a strength that is greater than my own. This is fortified by seeking out and finding reassurance from 'good deeds in a naughty world', which encourages the belief that goodness, courage, generosity and heroism are possible. This remains true even when such virtues are partially disclosed. There have been many lives like those of St. Francis, Gandhi and Schweitzer, which have shown how great is the human potential for heroic living. As I have already indicated, the life of Jesus does this for me and for many Friends, in an extremely powerful way.

In my religious quest I have found my association with the Society of Friends of enormous help. For Quakers have always held that their conviction that 'there is that of God in everyone' means that any person, whether a Christian or not, past, present or future, has the capacity to have the kind of experience I have been trying to describe in these pages. If people choose to use this capacity then they will come to know the experience that Quakers have called the 'inward light'. This can happen to everyone, whether or not they are Christians, in so far as they seek to realise this experience and, in its light, to live well and lovingly. In fact, many people who join the Society of Friends do so because they have already come intuitively to this awareness.

Quakers and the Bible

It is unlikely that this attitude to religious experience would have come about had Quakers accepted the Bible as the only source of religious authority, to be interpreted in a literal, fundamentalist manner. As I have already pointed out, early Friends knew and loved the scriptures, but they were also concerned to know the spirit that inspired them. Throughout Quaker history the Bible has continued to occupy a prominent place as a rich source of religious insight, which has resulted from the ways in which its authors have responded to the truth to be discovered in and through the business of living.

I am quite sure that many people are confused by the way in which some Christians (Friends among them) seem to imply that God is revealed in the Bible. They make it sound as if God dictates edicts, complete and whole, to chosen men like the prophets, whose job it was to pronounce them to their fellow men. Of course this is not the way in which informed Christians today understand biblical revelation. They would see the Bible, both Old and New Testaments, as a remarkable collection of writings covering the history and experience of countless, ordinary, fallible men and women, as individuals and in community, through a span of many hundreds of years. Among them have been people who had a great capacity to reflect upon the inwardness of this experience, and to interpret it to their fellows in such a way as to command respect for their insights, an interpretation of events and experiences which made sense to them, as disclosing a meaning and purpose that called for response in behaviour and action. These insights were of course expressed in the thought forms and assumptions of the day.

In this way a religious attitude and pattern of values were gradually developed. The authority of the Bible does not rest on an external and infallible guarantee of its truth, but on its ability to arouse the response and trust of people: to speak to their condition by its innate truthfulness. As Dr. Sandy, a famous biblical scholar said long ago in his Bampton Lectures, 'the test of inspiration is the capacity to inspire'.

So powerful has the influence of biblical literature been on the minds and lives of people, that for those who have responded to its insights it has seemed to disclose to them a knowledge of such fundamental importance, that they have felt compelled to describe it as knowledge of God: indeed many have spoken of a self-revelation or disclosure of God.

There is a wide acceptance among modern Quakers of this approach to the Bible, and I would like to underline two points which have particular importance for them. The first is the significant part that human response and interpretation have played in the development of biblical writings. This is why, in reading the Bible, we must always endeavour to get behind the letter of the text, and seek to discover the spirit that inspired its authors. We have also to be mindful of the part that the human element has played in the preservation, selection, editing and transmission of the text.

These recognitions account for the inconsistencies and uneven standard of the Bible. Nevertheless this approach enhances rather than detracts from its authority. Our response to the insights of the loftiest parts of the Bible commands our obedience to its message. We are glad of the scholarship and experience of people that have helped to make its message fully available to us.

This leads to my second point. People did not cease to be inspired and to feel the compulsion to interpret their history and experience when the canon of scripture was closed. Quakers see this as a continuing activity of people, as they seek to discover truth and to respond to it from whatever quarter it may arise.

It must however be frankly admitted that among modern Friends, the Bible, while still greatly treasured, is not so widely known as in previous generations. To some, and possibly to many Friends, this is a matter of regret, as they feel that, cut off from its roots in biblical literature and thinking, the life of the Society will wither. But I am personally convinced that where some of the time previously given to the study and devotional use of the Bible is spent on other sources of religious insight, the life of the Society will be enriched.

Quakers and creeds

It will be obvious from my attempts to describe the ways in which Quakers think about Jesus and approach the Bible, that their attitude to formal creeds and theological dogma is very different from that of most Christians. Friends have a deep dislike and distrust of credal statements as a basis for association in their fellowship. There are a variety of reasons for this, and the main one, as I have indicated earlier, is the Quaker awareness of the limitations of words to express the deepest human experiences, and the impossibility of defining them adequately.

Because of the importance Quakers place on personal integrity and sincerity in religious matters, they have realised that, while a form of words may suitably express personal convictions at one time, they will almost certainly be entirely unsuitable for the same person later in life. It is even more difficult to define the religious conviction of a group of people, and in order to accommodate them all, phrases that lend themselves to several interpretations have to be used. The position becomes well nigh impossible when people are expected to use statements made centuries earlier as the definition of their contemporary faith.

It often seems that one of the principal purposes of credal statements is to exclude people deemed to be heretics from association with a church, and this aspect strengthens Friends in their opposition to the use of creeds.

The absence of creeds does not mean that Quakers feel that it does not matter what a person believes, for they recognise that personal belief vitally affects the way in which people behave. Quakers are people of strong religious views, but they are quite clear that they must be tested by the way in which they are expressed in action. While many Friends have serious hesitations about the usefulness of theology, fearing that it leads too easily to speculation, all would agree that, as rational beings, we must think about the nature of our religious experience. Friends are encouraged, to seek for truth in all the opportunities that life presents to them. They are further encouraged, as I have indicated earlier, to seek new light from whatever quarter it may arise. Their questing, open attitude to life has certainly contributed to the tolerance with which Friends try to approach people and problems of faith and conduct.

It also makes it easier to understand how the Society can accommodate such a wide range of religious outlook among its members. Pretty well every colour in the theological spectrum is reflected in the views of Friends. There are those whose faith is most sincerely expressed in the traditional language of orthodox Christianity, as well as those who could fairly be described as religious humanists. Even in the Friend who is an orthodox Christian, elements of agnosticism are likely to lurk, and these become more marked as Friends range from right to left across the theological scale.

In between these two positions are Friends who would find it hard to be articulate about their faith, but if pressed would be likely to say that their aim was to live in the spirit of loving trust so clearly demonstrated by Jesus.

Quaker guidelines

The above paragraphs may present a somewhat bewildering picture of the beliefs held by individual Quakers but they are not left on their own in finding their religious attitudes to life.

From the earliest years of the Society, Friends have found it desirable to draw together writings that reflect the corporate, as well as the individual experience of Friends in their religious quest, and to publish them as a *Book of Christian Discipline*, so that they may be easily available. From time to time the contents of this book are carefully revised by the whole Society, so that it reflects as far as possible the contemporary attitudes of Friends. It is published in two parts: *Christian Faith and Practice in the experience of the Society of Friends* (revised in 1959) and *Church Government** (revised 1967).

The opening section of *Christian Faith and Practice* consists of 'extracts illustrating the spiritual experience of many Friends, from George Fox to the present time'. The rest of the book covers the convictions and attitude of the Society on a wide variety of subjects which arise out of their mutual experience.

The Society also addresses to its members *Advices and Queries*† (revised in 1964), the purpose of which is to remind them of the general Quaker outlook in a succinct manner. The method of presentation is well illustrated by the first three Queries, which ask: 'Do you cherish that of God within you that his love and power may grow in you and rule your life?' 'Do you seek to follow Jesus, who shows us the Father, and is himself the Way?' 'Is your religion rooted in personal experience of God? How does it find expression in your life?'

These publications have made an important contribution to the life of the Society, by setting out its corporate understanding of the religious interpretation of life. Individual Friends have undoubtedly found in them sources of strength and encouragement, and valuable signposts that are helpful to them in their own seeking. These collections of corporate writings are not laid on Friends as authoritative statements for unquestioning acceptance: rather they are presented as useful guidelines. They command the respect of Friends because they are drawn from the actual experience of the Society, in the past and in the present, and because each Friend in each generation has the opportunity to participate in reformulating them.

---

*See page 48

† Included in *Church Government* and also issued as a pamphlet.

One of the most remarkable features of the Society of Friends is that it has been able to hold in unity within its fellowship people who are strongly individualistic and those who are strongly gregarious; people who are seekers but who are not afraid to commit themselves to what they find. The strength of Quakerism lies in a continuous seeking together by its members for love and truth, and in their willing response and loyalty to what is discovered in this corporate exploration. In their seeking and finding Quakers recognise the profound meaning of the New Testament phrase, 'we love because he first loved us'.*

* *John* iv, 19.

3

QUAKER WORSHIP

To my mind the most effective way in which Quakers participate in the life of the Society is through sharing regularly in Quaker Meetings for Worship. Quakers go to their Meetings not primarily from a sense of duty, but because they want and need to do so; for this reason the Meeting for Worship is the core of the Society's life. To the Meeting for Worship Friends may contribute the insight that arises from their varied experience of life. Through the Meeting for Worship they can find a reinforcement of the strength and courage required for living, and a source of enlightenment which will be of tremendous importance to them in trying to find their way in daily life.

These, I realise, are strong claims to make, but they seem to me fully justified by the experience of Friends. They are certainly true of Quaker worship at its best, and it is at this level that I shall present it. Like all living experiences, Quaker worship cannot be adequately described: the only way to find out what it is like is to take part in an actual Meeting. Furthermore, in writing about Quaker worship, I shall inevitably use images that have particular meaning for me, and I fully realise that other Friends would use different images to describe an experience which is real to us all. It is hardly necessary to point out that there can be no guarantee that a Meeting for Worship will automatically succeed. Each Meeting must be seen, in some ways, as an act of faith in personal relationships and an experiment in a religious search. Much depends on the full and sincere participation of all present, and on the spirit of expectancy in which they come to Meeting.

The central activity

Like the name 'Society of Friends' for the body of Quakers, that of 'Meeting for Worship' for their central activity is not accidental; it means exactly what it says. Quakers are a community of people who love and care for one another, and their central activity is, at one level, a meeting together to acknowledge the worth of, and to be influenced by, the religious values they hold in common. It is also significant that the name of the place where the Meeting is held has a home-like sound about it, for it is called a Meeting House and not a church or chapel. Where Friends do not own premises they meet in a hired room, for Quaker Meetings do not require consecrated buildings: they can just as well be held in a private home, and sometimes are. Quaker Meetings can be arranged at any time of the day, and on any day of the week, but it is generally most convenient to hold them on a Sunday and usually in the morning.

The furnishings of the room are simple. The seats, generally benches in an old Meeting House or chairs in a modern one, are arranged in a circle, or hollow square or oblong, with a table in the centre. There is no altar, pulpit or organ. Hymns are not sung or prayer books used, and there is no ordered form of service or liturgy.

Unfortunately, it is widely thought that Quaker Meetings are closed gatherings for members only. This is quite false. Anyone who wishes to attend is warmly welcomed, and is encouraged to take a full part in the Meeting.

The start of Meeting

A Meeting begins when the first person arrives, sits down and waits quietly in silence. Others enter the room and share in the stillness. People come to a Quaker Meeting as individuals but their aim is to achieve a sense of communion with others present through being open to them in an attitude of friendship, sympathy and understanding. Earlier in this essay I described the experience that arises from a journey into the interior of our being. Here at the deepest place, we find a quiet, still centre, where we are most vividly aware of ourselves as individuals, and also of our relationship to others. The quietness of a Quaker Meeting provides an ideal setting for the exploration of the most profound levels of our existence, and also the realisation of our loving relationship with others present. Encounters with people in such depth take us all into a dimension different from that of ordinary living. It is worth recalling that the early Friends spoke of the first part of a Meeting for Worship as 'centering down'. We experience a heightened perception, in which we know that we have discovered and been discovered by a love that renews and invigorates our whole being. The setting of this experience is the meeting together and loving encounter between people, but it points to a source of light and love which, while beyond, is yet near. Friends have never hesitated to accept this as an experience of God.

Because a Quaker Meeting is essentially a spontaneous dynamic growing relationship, it is impossible to prescribe a pattern for it, except in the most general way. In any Meeting that is really alive there will certainly develop a sense of awe and wonder akin to that which grows in us as we are warmed by the experience of deep human love. One inevitable consequence of being loved by someone is to feel a sense of our utter unworthiness of that love, and yet at the same time to be able to accept ourselves as we are because we have been accepted. So love re-creates us and releases in us the potential of our being. In a not dissimilar way, this too can happen to us in worship. When it does, it brings a sense of gratitude, harmony and thankfulness which colours the atmosphere of the Meeting, for we make our own the faith of the first Christians that God is love.

So the Meeting proceeds for about an hour, growing in sensitivity and power towards a state where those present experience a profound and deep communion. One early Friend well expressed the result of his experience by saying that '. . . when I came into the silent assemblies of God's people, I felt a secret power among them, which touched my heart; and as I gave way unto it I found the evil weakening in me and the good raised up . . .'

Spoken contributions

From time to time Quaker Meetings will be entirely silent, and such Meetings can be extraordinarily powerful. These are rather exceptional. There are usually some brief spoken contributions, traditionally referred to as 'ministry'. The purpose is twofold. Whatever is said should seek to reflect the deep spiritual awareness present in the Meeting. It should be, as the old Quaker phrase has it, 'in the life'. The second purpose of a spoken contribution is that it ought to have as its aim the spontaneous building up of the actual life of the Meeting itself. So specially prepared sermons or exhortations have no place in a Meeting.

The kind of ministry that is valued is that which is drawn from the real experience of the speakers—something that they have made their own because it has been hammered out on the anvil of life. They will speak in their own words and use their own ideas, nevertheless what is spoken will be said on behalf of all present and accepted by them because the speaker has been sensitive to the spirit of the Meeting.

No provision is made for set readings from the Bible, but when a passage is spontaneously chosen for its appropriateness to the requirements of a particular Meeting, it can be a most helpful way of contributing to its life. Readings in Meeting are not limited to those from the Bible, and any suitable book can be used. There is a practical difficulty here, for while most Meetings have a Bible on the table, other books are not so easily available. Bringing them to Meetings smacks of a degree of planning that is not usually helpful. There is one exception in that many Meetings still follow the practice of reading selec-

A playscheme for mentally and physically handicapped children run by young volunteers from Belgium, England, Germany, Holland, Ireland, Poland, Morocco and Sudan. Many similar workcamps are organised each year by the Quaker Work Camps Committee.

Wanstead Meeting House, London, opened 1968 (Photo: Colin Westwood)

Preparing to televise a Quaker meeting for worship from Come-to-Good, Cornwall (Photo: T. P. Roskrow)

Meeting for worship at Kingston, Surrey (Photo: Noeline Kelly)

tions from the *Advices and Queries* during the period of worship, although a number prefer to arrange for such readings after the Meeting itself has closed.

It is hoped that all Meetings will be held in a prayerful manner, in the sense that those present will be open to the life of the spirit. Sometimes however, though more rarely now than in previous generations, a spoken prayer will be offered. As in ministry, it will be a spontaneous contribution, arising in response to the deep life of the Meeting. Anyone who attends a Meeting, man or woman, Friend or not, is free to speak, pray or read, provided always that he or she is moved to do so through sensitivity to the spirit in the gathering.

Variety of approach

There is no technique of Quaker worship, and those present will follow the way which is most natural to them. I once asked a young Friend what she did when she first settled in Meeting. She said she looked round the Meeting and was deeply thankful that there were so many people present who really loved her and whom she loved. This appealed to me as an excellent starting point for a Meeting. Other Friends will probably make use of some form of meditation and contemplation they find personally helpful.

For many Friends present the focus of the Meeting will be their awareness of the living presence of Jesus, through the recollection of incidents in his life or of something that he said which is specially meaningful to them. In fact this is the main reason why Quakers have never observed, in an outward form, the sacrament of Holy Communion. To symbolise the presence of Jesus by the use of bread and wine seemed unnecessary because in their quiet Meetings they were vividly aware of his real presence with them.

I have written at some length on the Quaker Meeting for Worship because of the important place it occupies in the life of the Society of Friends. In doing so I realise that I may well have given the impression that Friends attending Meeting always enjoy a powerful and illuminating spiritual experience, in which their attention is unwaveringly and deeply concentrated. Sometimes this does happen to me, but, more frequently than I would wish, I find I catch but fleeting glimpses of the profound depths which I know are possible. Often this is my fault, but sometimes it is not, for the Meeting itself is not truly gathered together. Sometimes my mind wanders over an amazing variety of fascinating subjects, some of which are far from what a 'proper' Quaker should be contemplating in Meeting!

Experience of Meeting

My most common experience of Meeting can best be described by again using the analogy of personal friendship. Being in the company of a deeply loved friend gives a sense of relaxation and warmth which arises from mutual trust. I shall not be continually thinking in a conscious way about the nature of our friendship, but at a deeper level I am aware of its value. Quite simply I accept it and enjoy it. Nothing very dramatic may happen while we are together, although sometimes we may reach an unexpected new level of awareness and understanding. Probably much of our time has been spent in silence, for one sign of a real friendship is the ability to be together in quietness without embarrassment. Always I look back on the occasion of our meeting with a sense that I am a better person because of it—I have been enriched by the experience.

To develop human friendship requires effort and persistence and the exercise of patience and understanding—you cannot get to know someone you never take the trouble to meet, and you will only come to know your friend as the result of many meetings. Whilst it would be wrong to press the analogy of the experience of personal friendship too far, I think it will serve to illustrate my point: that to achieve the benefit of a Quaker Meeting does require effort and persistence, but in the end yields a rich reward for the effort made. Charles Lamb the essayist, not himself a Friend, wrote of Friends' way of worship: '. . . would'st thou know what true peace and quiet mean; would'st thou find a refuge from the noises and clamours of the multitude; would'st thou enjoy at once solitude and society; would'st thou possess the depth of thy own spirit in stillness, without being shut out from the consolatory faces of thy species; would'st thou be alone, and yet accompanied; solitary, yet not desolate; singular, yet not without some to keep thee in countenance; a unit in aggregate; a simple in composite:—come with me into a Quaker's Meeting.*'

Children and Quaker worship

A question frequently asked by people who are interested in Quakerism is how children cope with silent worship. Most Friends do not expect their children to sit through an hour's Meeting, and provision is made, where possible, for groups that will cater for their requirements in rooms on the premises. The particular arrangements will be adapted to the ages of the children, and will range from doing things with paint and plasticine, through stories of a varied kind, to work projects, play-acting and discussion groups for the young teenagers. Children are accepted as an integral part of the local Quaker community, and the time they are together provides an excellent chance for the older Friends looking after them to get to know them as persons, and to build up friendship with them.

The opportunity will also be taken to inform the children about the Quaker understanding of Christianity and to introduce them to Friends' attitudes in general. This will be done in an objective manner, and will strenuously avoid any tinge of indoctrination which Quakers abhor. Because of this, some parents who are not themselves Quakers send their children to the Meeting House so that they can share in these activities.

---

*Charles Lamb (1775-1834) A Quaker's Meeting in *The Essays of Elia*. London: Oxford Univ. Press (World Classics), 1946, p.65

These local efforts for children and teenagers will be supplemented by summer schools and camps, and by day regional gatherings.

It is recognised that the primary responsibility for the religious education of children rests with their parents. The Society asks in the eleventh Query: 'Do those of you who are parents seek to share your deepest beliefs with your children, while leaving them free to develop as the Spirit of God may lead them?'

From what I have already written about the Meeting for Worship it is clear that in this central Quaker activity Friends find one of the most valuable sources of religious insight and strength. It would be strange indeed if they denied this to their children. In fact, all children are given the opportunity to spend a short time in Meeting itself. This will be either at the start, or towards the close of the Meeting. In this way it is hoped that children will gain first-hand experience in the practice of silent worship and gradually come to appreciate it. I believe that children get much more out of this way of worship than is generally supposed, and I know some Quaker parents keep their children with them throughout the whole hour.

Whether children come in for all or for part of a Meeting, I think it can fairly be claimed that Quakers enjoy having children about, as their presence makes more real the sense of community which it is important that the Meeting should encourage.

Quakers and the after-life

Because Quaker attitudes to life after death are vitally affected by their experience of worship this is a suitable place to touch briefly on this subject.

The hope of life after death has never been considered as a reward for virtue, nor as a compensation for adversity. Neither has the fear of damnation been used as a threat to induce godly living. Such ideas are wholly repugnant to Quakers.

The Quaker view of what happens beyond death is firmly rooted in their experience of this life. They affirm passionately their conviction that life is good, and that an essential clue to its real nature is to be glimpsed in the love that people have for one another. There is always an element of mystery about love which people cannot fully penetrate, but Quakers are convinced that it has a timeless quality, and that it always points to a mystery beyond itself. Death cannot destroy this love; it is not limited by time and space.

This conviction is underlined by their experience of Quaker worship at its best, and by their awareness that the personality of Jesus was not diminished by his death, for his life was based on his profound trust that God is love. Quakers know that as they respond to this love they experience 'heaven' now, and that whatever lies beyond death must be for man's good.

So Quakers do not dogmatise about what happens after death. There are Friends who are convinced that there is an after-life, and those who are convinced that there is not. All Friends feel that it is more important to get on with living this life, and seek to improve the conditions of people in this world than to engage in speculations about the next.

Quaker funerals are essentially Meetings for worship with the particular purpose of giving thanks for the way in which the love of God has been expressed in the life of the deceased Friend. They are also opportunities for loving support and sympathy to the bereaved. Now that cremation has become so widely accepted among Friends it is usual for a brief Meeting for Worship attended by the family and a few Friends to be held at the crematorium. This can be followed if desired at a later time by a 'memorial' Meeting for Worship at the Meeting House. Elaborate mourning and extravagant expenditure on wreaths is clearly out of place, for the Quaker funeral is an occasion for simple thankfulness.

My aim in this chapter has been to describe Quaker worship, as far as possible in words and thought forms that are in everyday use, so that people can see that worship is not a strange, other-worldly activity but something which can have meaning for them and to which they can relate.

The chapter could equally well have been written in more traditional language. In that case I would have said that Quakers go to meetings so that together they can meet God and acknowledge the worth of his love. By this love we are re-created and made whole for it is in God that 'we live and move, in him we exist'.*

In worship that of God in me discovers that of God in others, and we are drawn into a holy communion as we respond to the spirit of God in whose presence we meet.

---

* *Acts* xvii, 28 (NEB).

4

THE QUAKER COMMUNITY

In this book I have used the word 'Meeting' in two ways, and in doing so have covered two different uses to which it is put by Quakers. In the first it refers to the activity of Quaker worship. In the second it is used in a collective sense to refer to the company of people who form the community of Friends in a particular locality.

If the high claims that Friends make for their way of silent worship are to be justified and the method itself vindicated, it must be seen to produce and foster a quality of individual and community life in those who participate in Meetings for Worship week by week. Because in its method Quaker worship draws so heavily on the practice of personal relationships, the quality of the fellowship realised among Friends obviously has a direct bearing on the depth of the life of the Meeting for Worship. Quaker worship and the life of the Quaker community are inextricably intertwined.

It is the aim of every Meeting to become an open, loving community of people, who care for one another, and because of their attitude of trustful acceptance, give significance and support to one another. In such a community loneliness is banished, and life is shown to be good for people are accepted, loved and valued for what they are, and themselves seek to love and respect others.

Friends of course often fail to achieve this high standard, but it remains their objective. They are strengthened in their intention by the memory of over 300 years of Quaker history, and by their present experience, that in their worship and personal religious life, there is a source of loving power that continually supports them.

Personal friendships

In the pursuit and development of such a community Friends naturally place great emphasis on the importance of ordinary friendship. In the many claims on a Quaker's time, that of making friends among members of the Meeting has high priority. This objective is most effectively achieved in the first place through a variety of informal social relationships, springing from personal affinities among people of similar tastes and interests. You start with the people you like, and gradually seek to widen the circle of your personal friends.

In most Meetings there will usually be a number of such overlapping circles. It is not expected that Friends will immediately like all the other members of their Meeting: it is however assumed that they will try to love them. I realise that a lot of Friends may not like some of my views and attitudes, or share my likes and dislikes, just as I do not care for some of their activities and interests. Nevertheless, I know that I can count on their love, by which I mean their acceptance, loyalty, support, respect for, and trust in me as a person, just as they can count on mine.

Corporate activities

Complementing these ordinary expressions of human friendship, will be certain activities arranged by the Meeting as a corporate body, which aim to foster the fellowship of the Meeting as a whole. These will vary tremendously, according to the needs and numbers of Friends and their geographic distribution. They will almost certainly include at some time the arrangement of groups for discussion and study, which have the twofold purpose, first, of helping to keep people associated with the Meeting informed about the rational content of Quaker belief and Christian thinking, and attitudes to modern problems, second, of helping people to get to know one another.

Alongside such groups will be others concerned with a wide range of activities which can stretch from work projects to maintain the premises, through the holding of austerity lunches to raise funds for charity, to a visit to a theatre, such as happened in my own Meeting, when the daughter of one of our members was the principal boy in a pantomime. For fear that it should be assumed that Quaker communal life is cluttered with a host of organised activities, let me hasten to point out that Friends have a dislike of arranging events which members feel obliged to attend, just for the sake of doing so. Whatever activities are held are arranged in accordance with the wishes of Friends.

In my attempt to give a picture of the kind of corporate life that may be expected in a Meeting I have naturally referred almost entirely to Friends. It is now necessary to emphasise that people who are not Friends, but would like to share in any of these activities, are warmly welcomed. Quakerism involves an attitude of friendliness and sympathy to all people, and consequently Quakers are encouraged to make personal friendships as widely as possible among the people they meet in all the spheres in which they move outside the Society. In so doing they incidentally become more interesting and lively people themselves, and also help to fulfil the desire of the Meeting to be an open community. This in fact is the only way in which it can live, for any group that attempts to preserve its life in isolation is doomed to extinction.

What kind of people?

In a body like the Society of Friends, which welcomes variety, and encourages individuality, it is not easy to give a brief, accurate and inclusive description of the kind of people likely to be associated with it. But most Friends could be described as people who enjoy thinking things out for themselves.

In earlier times Quakers were apt to frown on many forms of entertainment as worldly and time-wasting. But present-day Friends realise that the cinema, television, radio, music and the theatre can be valuable and creative ways to enlarge their experience.

Quakers can hardly be described as extravagant, and their mode of living is characterised by a sensible simplicity. There was a time when the Society was self-consciously following an asceticism that produced an unfortunate dowdiness, especially in the way members dressed. This has now passed, and while not slavishly dragooned by every whim of fashion, both men and women dress sensibly in modern clothes. Women Friends use make up if they wish.

There was a time too when many Friends were teetotallers in protest against the excessive popular use of alcohol. In 1964, when the Society was revising the Advices, account had to be taken of the views of those who were convinced teetotallers, and those who enjoyed drinking in moderation. Unity was reached in the following words, 'In view of the evils arising from the unwise use of alcohol, tobacco and other habit-forming drugs, consider how far you should limit your use of them or whether you should refrain from them altogether'.

Quaker occupations

Any Meeting is certain to include a considerable contingent of housewives, and also a substantial group of people who live by similar practical skills. Among other contributions they provide an invaluable down-to-earth commonsense element in the Society's life.

Friends tend to follow occupations that directly stem from their interest in people. Teachers and educationalists abound, and there is a fast-growing representation of every variety of social worker. Quakers are to be found in all branches of the medical profession, and their experimental approach to religion and life has drawn a large number of Quakers into scientific work.

Business tycoons are almost entirely absent, but there are still Friends who run their own businesses. A good many Quakers are engaged in banking, accountancy and industry, and there is a smattering of trade union officials. Some Friends are farmers and horticulturists. Professional politicians are at a low ebb at the present time, but a number of Friends work in local government and in the civil service.

The Quaker approach to religion is essentially practical, and they always want to test their faith by the way it works out in everyday life, because this, in their view, is the sphere where real, true religious faith can be seen to be relevant by the way in which it is expressed. It has often been said that Quakerism is a way of life. The Quaker attitude is well summed up in the seventeenth Query: 'Do you carry through faithfully all the responsibilities entrusted to you? Are you conscientious in your daily work? Do you dwell too much on the hope of recognition or reward? When pressure is brought to bear upon you to lower your standards, are you prepared to resist it?'

I have sometimes been criticised for seeming to suggest that the Society is a kind of friendly club of like-minded people which is so open and tolerant that anyone can believe what they like and do anything they desire.

This is certainly not how I see the Quaker community. In my view it is the primary area in which Friends apply their trust in and conviction about God. We try to follow Jesus in his trust that God is love: but no one will accept that we do so unless we demonstrated the reality of our faith by the loving quality of the Quaker community. In so doing we are fulfilling the New Testament exhortation 'to love one another for love is of God'.

The love demanded of Quakers (and of all Christians) is the most demanding, costly and sacrificial requirement that can be asked of human beings. As we commit ourselves to love's demands we find that we are responding to a love that is already there.

5

QUAKER ORGANISATION

So far I have been describing the Quaker community at the level of individuals who share in it. Like all communities it functions at several levels, and something must now be said about the way in which a local Meeting is organised. In view of the basic outlook of Friends, it will come as no surprise that the organsiation of the Society is democratic, is kept as simple as possible, and that men and women share in it equally.

No mention has been made of clergy and ministers, for there are none. From the start of the Society, Friends did not set aside some of their number as a separated, ordained ministry, to conduct their worship or to act as organisers of their corporate life. In 300 years Quakers in this country have found that this arrangement has worked well, and they have had no cause to change it. Leadership in the Quaker community will be focused in Friends whose experience, sensitivity and wisdom qualify them for particular service to the Meeting. Their authority arises from the fact that their fellow Friends recognise the value of their experience and of the gifts they have to offer; it is not conferred upon them by their appointment to an office. But as there is always the danger that jobs left to everybody may be done by none, certain Friends, because of their suitability, are appointed to a limited number of offices to ensure that the total life of the Quaker community functions adequately.

Probably the most obvious of these Friends will be those who sit, as the old Quaker phrase has it, at 'the head of Meeting'—nowadays generally some central place in the group. It is a handshake between two of them that records the formal close of the Meeting for Worship. From the early days of the Society such Friends have been known as 'Elders'. Their duty is to feel a particular responsibility for the spiritual life of the members, and to encourage the right holding of Meetings for Worship.

A related office is that of the Overseer, whose special responsibility is directed toward the more practical aspects of the life of the Quaker community. Friends serving in either of these capacities will be available to give advice to members when it is required, and to take initiative to ensure that practical assistance is rendered when needed. Elders and Overseers are not necessarily expected to provide all the help and advice, but to make certain that it is easily available from the most suitable source. Both men and women are eligible for these offices and they are appointed for a three-year period.

Preparative and Monthly Meetings

At the close of each Meeting for Worship a Friend, man or woman, generally gives out notices of forthcoming events likely to be of interest to people in the Meeting. This Friend is the Meeting's Clerk, who on this occasion is acting in the capacity of a secretary to the Meeting. At regular periods throughout the year, as often as is required, business meetings are held. These are open to all members associated with the local group of Friends. The Clerk presides over these gatherings in a capacity akin to that of chairman and secretary. Sometimes these meetings follow the Meeting for Worship, or they can be held at any convenient time during the week. Known as 'Preparative Meetings', they are the instrument by which the group of Friends decides on the activities it wishes to undertake for its own purposes, or in the local community, and also deals with such practical matters as the maintenance of the Meeting's premises. Another important function of Preparative Meeting is to appoint some Friends to attend the area business meetings of the Society, called Monthly Meetings, because at one time they were held each month. The timing of these meetings is now adjusted in the light of the volume of work to be done. I know a

Monthly Meeting that has so ordered its business that it functions adequately with six meetings a year.

Monthly Meetings are the primary business meetings in the Society, and among their powers are those of admitting new members into the Society—so Friend's membership of the Society is through a Monthly Meeting, usually the one in their area of residence. Monthly Meeting is the focal point for the discussion of Quaker affairs in the locality, and also of issues which its members desire to be considered by the Society. Elders and Overseers are appointed by Monthly Meetings, which have overall responsibility for the general life of the Society in their areas.

The method used by Monthly Meeting in conducting its affairs is the same as that followed in all Quaker business meetings. It gathers in an atmosphere of silent worship, and all that has been said about that important aspect of Quaker life applies to Monthly Meetings, which are therefore much more than just opportunities for transacting business, for they are among the ways in which the Society builds up its corporate life, and discovers its common mind.

Business procedure

No vote is taken in Quaker business meetings, as the method of reaching a truthful and right decision by counting heads is clearly inconsistent with the Quaker emphasis on the value of people as unique individuals, and of their relationship with one another. Although voting may appear to achieve quick results, it frequently does so at the cost of allowing a majority to ride roughshod over the views of a minority. Quakers would rather defer action if they are unable to reach a united decision. This may slow the pace but it does help to ensure that when decisions are reached they will command the respect and loyal support of everyone.

Quaker business procedure is simple. A matter calling for a decision will be presented briefly by the Clerk, or by a Friend who feels a concern for it. Friends will listen quietly and with sympathy to these introductory words, and weigh them carefully in their minds. The matter is then before the Meeting, and all are free to contribute to the exercise of discovering what is the right course of action. In simple issues, which clearly have the support of all present, this is made explicit by two or three Friends voicing the agreement of all in such cryptic traditional Quaker phrases as 'I hope that will be done', or more simply, 'I agree'. Where the matter is more complicated various Friends in the room will state their convictions and views, trying to avoid language that is likely to be provocative or hurtful. Friends, being human, do not always fulfil this counsel of perfection. If there is an obvious conflict of view, the Clerk may call for a period of silence during which no spoken contributions are made, so that in quietness Friends can be specially sensitive to the 'leadings of the Spirit'. After this time of waiting further discussion takes place and gradually a common view will emerge. As the result of this searching process the original concern may be modified and will almost certainly be enriched. It is the duty of the Clerk to gauge 'the sense of the Meeting' and to record it in a written minute which is read aloud, so that it can be amended by those present until it is felt to be an adequate expression of the decision they have reached.

National organisation

Matters that are felt to need consideration by the whole Society are considered in the manner described above, and are then forwarded to 'London Yearly Meeting', which is the annual gathering of all Friends in Britain, and British Friends' final policy-making body. Alternatively, especially if it is an urgent issue, it can be referred to 'Meeting for Sufferings'—the Society's Executive Committee which meets monthly. The name comes from the time in the seventeenth century, when Quakers were bitterly persecuted for their faith, and a committee was set up to deal with their sufferings. Both these bodies can refer issues to Monthly Meetings for consideration or action.

General Meetings comprise all the Monthly Meetings in a region. They gather two or three times a year, and are mainly opportunities for fellowship and for general consideration of all aspects of Quaker life. Their executive powers are limited.

Friends accept the necessity for the Society's simple, democratic organisation which aims to involve them all in policy and decision making. Without it the Society of Friends could not exist as an organised body which supports and guides its members and various local Meetings, and when necessary expresses their views as a corporate body, or takes action on their behalf.

Friends are not expected to attend every business meeting that is open to them. The amount of service that members render in this way will vary according to the circumstances in which they find themselves at different times of their lives. This flexible system has worked well and the Society has always been able to count on sufficient numbers of Friends who are able and willing to support its business meetings.

A simple organisation is never the result of casual, slipshod arrangements. Through the years Friends have given a great deal of careful thought to the most suitable mode for the Society's organisation, so that it will be efficient and at the same time flexible, simple and spontaneous. The details of its organisation and procedure are set out in *Church Government* (last revised in 1967) which forms the second part of the *Book of Christian Discipline*, to which reference was made on page 27.

Quaker marriage

It may seem strange to introduce the subject of marriage at this point, but arrangements for the conduct of marriages have to comply with the law, and therefore call for regulations to be laid down by the Society.

Quaker marriages are recognised in law, and each Monthly Meeting appoints one of its number as a Registering Officer. It is their responsibility to ensure that the requirements of the law are met, that the Society's regulations have been complied with, and that proper records are kept.

The marriage is solemnised in a Meeting House during a Meeting for Worship specially appointed for the purpose. In the course of the Meeting the couple will rise and the man will make the following declaration, 'Friends, I take this my Friend C.D. to be my wife, promising through divine assistance, to be unto her a loving and faithful husband, so long as we both on earth shall live'. The woman makes a similar promise as his wife. The Meeting continues with ministry or prayer as individuals present are moved to speak. At some point before the close of the Meeting the couple sign a certificate which includes the wording of the declarations they have made. It is witnessed by at least two of those present, and is then read aloud by the Registering Officer. At the conclusion of the Meeting all present at the marriage who have heard the declarations are invited to sign the certificate. The couple also sign the Civil Register.

Monthly Meetings can if they think it appropriate allow Quaker marriage procedure to be used by non-Friends, and are also given discretion whether or not to grant permission for the marriage in a Meeting House of a couple, of whom one or both have been divorced.

On a subject as controversial as divorce it is not surprising that there is some diversity of view among Friends, but many would accept the attitude reflected in the words of a report prepared and published by the direction of Yearly Meeting some years ago.

Having set out the high Quaker view of marriage the report states, '. . . we must recognise, in humility and without censure, that human failures do occur. The reasons for such failures do not necessarily lie in the poverty of a couple's spiritual reserves, nor in their neglecting to seek the help of God in overcoming the times of difficulty and disillusionment which arise in every marriage. No couple, marrying with any deep conviction of permanence, would willingly give up the struggle to overcome their difficulties and seek a way of escape. But where the difficulties involved in a marriage are, of their very nature, serving to drive a couple further apart in bitterness of mind and heart, or where they reduce them to an empty and conventional semblance of living together, then there can be little reason for keeping within the bonds of legal marriage two people between whom no spiritual marriage exists. Broken marriages are always a calamity, but particularly so if there are children, since they need above all a stable home and the love and care of both parents.'*

* *The Marriage Relationship*, London: Friends Book Centre, 1949, p. 20 (out of print)

6
QUAKER CONCERNS

A word from the Quaker past which is still in current use in the Society today is 'concern'. It means that a Friend, or group of Friends, feel a deep sense of religious compulsion, more powerful than a strong inclination, to carry out some action. Quakers are convinced that to be valid a religious outlook must always seek ways in which it can be translated into practice.

This conviction will be characteristic of every Quaker Meeting, although the kind of service they can carry out in their locality will vary greatly according to the size of the Meeting, and the availability of its members. The easiest way to illustrate the sort of activities a local Meeting may carry out is to mention some things that have actually been done. Meetings have invited groups of overseas students to a variety of social gatherings so that they could meet people in the neighbourhood. Many Meetings have arranged 'bread and cheese' lunches to raise funds for Quaker overseas service, Oxfam, etc. A number of Meetings have been responsible for street collections for Christian Aid, and many Meeting Houses have been used as collection centres for clothes for refugees. Members of a Meeting I know well have for years visited lonely patients in a ward for chronically sick people in a local hospital, and the Meeting raises money for Christmas presents for them.

Personal service

While many Meetings are likely to be involved in some corporate activities, most of the service to the local community will be given by Friends in their individual capacity or through a variety of voluntary agencies. Friends have a longstanding interest in prisoners, and a Quaker 'chaplain' is appointed to most large prisons, while many Friends act as prison visitors. A not inconsiderable number of Friends serve as Justices of the Peace. There is a strong interest in the Samaritan movement, and the work of the Marriage Guidance Council has attracted Friends, especially its counselling aspects.

Because of Quakers' particular interest in peace and international relations it is natural that they will gravitate to local organisations like the United Nations Association or Amnesty International. Friends have often taken the initiative in sponsoring activities to promote such causes as the campaign against torture and for disarmament. The Quaker concern for education has led some Friends into the Workers Educational Association, and others into more individual work such as teaching English to immigrants and helping them to adapt to life in this country. While there are few youth clubs directly sponsored by Meetings, a number of Friends engage in youth work of one kind or another. Quakers are specially sensitive to the problems facing children who are physically handicapped or emotionally deprived, and a considerable and growing number of Friends are involved in this demanding area of service.

The increasing emphasis on party politics in local and county councils has proved somewhat uncongenial to Quakers, and my impression is that fewer take part in these activities than was the case a generation ago, but there are still many Quakers to be found on such bodies.

Most Meetings appoint representatives to local councils of churches, and are especially happy to share in their practical work. Some Meetings have sponsored housing associations for the elderly and other groups, such as ex-prisoners for which accommodation is a pressing need. Friends have also co-operated in similar schemes initiated by Christian councils or other bodies.

Features of Quaker service

Certain typical features of Quaker local service emerge from this brief survey, one being the difficulty of drawing a sharp distinction between the corporate service of a Meeting and that of its individual members. It is also obvious that Friends tend to be attracted to service that involves them directly with people. Meetings are wary of assuming the organisation of social work that could better be done by professionally trained people, or that which should be the responsibility of the local community itself. My personal knowledge of the Society leads me to the view that Meetings and Friends are often quickly sensitive to particular local needs, and are prepared to take the initiative in demonstrating how they can be met. To achieve this they may well carry through a pilot scheme, which attracts the interest of other people, and so becomes woven into the community service of the neighbourhood. Friends will continue to share in the concern but do not seek to retain control of it beyond the preliminary stages.

One final point that must be spelt out is that, while Quakers would not describe their motives and actions in high-sounding moral terms, they would all recognise that they are the natural outcome of their response to the experience of God as love, discovered deep within them, and which is nurtured in the community of Friends and in their common sharing in silent worship.

7
NATIONAL ACTIVITIES

I have dealt at some length with the life and activities of Friends at the local level because this is where all Friends participate in the Society's life. It is also the place where people becoming interested in Friends will have their actual experience of Quakerism. While the life of the Society is mainly focused in its local Meetings, it also exists as a nationwide, and indeed as a world-wide, body. There are, of course, many issues on which Friends as a corporate Society will want to make their views known, as there are also particular things it feels it must do, which could not easily be achieved by local groups. For these reasons the Society has established, under Meeting for Sufferings, three departments and various committees which have responsibility for particular Quaker interests and concerns.

Naturally these are similar to those that are found in local Meetings. The roots of some can be traced back to the early days of the Society. Others have developed over the years in response to changing conditions and the desire of Friends to respond quickly to current needs within the Society itself, in the nation and in the world at large.

All the work carried out by Quakers corporately is a practical expression of their religious convictions, that is nurtured in the life and worship of the Society. It complements the work of individual Friends in their daily life and also of those who are directly involved in charitable or local authority services.

For several years the Society has been taking a fresh look at the various aspects of its work which is based in its London headquarters at Friends House. The object of the review has been to try to evolve a structure that would demonstrate the unity of all Quaker work and also rationalise its organisation.

With this end in mind three departments were set up in 1978 to draw together related pieces of service, formerly carried out by the Friends Education Council, the Friends Home Service Committee, the Friends Service Council, the Peace and International Relations Committee, and the Social Responsibility Council. They are Quaker Home Service, Quaker Peace and Service, and Quaker Social Responsibility and Education. These departments include representatives from Monthly Meetings, together with other Friends who share the special concern for the work they are charged to carry out on behalf of the whole Society. In the following paragraphs I propose to indicate the broad outlines of the kinds of service that Friends try to do corporately. Some of it organised locally some nationally.

Education

Quakers have always had a strong concern for education in the widest sense, following on their conviction that there is 'that of God in everyone'. Consequently, they believe that education should ultimately be seen as a religious activity aiming at the fullest possible development of the potentialities of human personality. This view is reflected in the high proportion of Friends who are engaged in almost all aspects of education. The majority of Quaker teachers work in state schools, but some teach in the Society's nine boarding schools. Six are co-educational; two are primarily for boys and one is for girls. Their staffs and scholars include Quakers and non-Quakers, and their endeavour is to create a relaxed atmosphere of friendliness, in which children may discover themselves as persons in their own right. While academic achievement is respected and encouraged, it is not treated as the sole aim of the schools, which seek to foster the development of the whole personality, and to this end great emphasis is placed on the encouragement of artistic, musical and practical skills. Friends have always approached education in a flexible and experimental manner and several individual Quakers have founded 'progressive' schools.

In the field of adult education is Woodbrooke, around which has developed an unique federated group of colleges in Selly Oak, Birmingham. Woodbrooke is a residential college providing a wide range of studies covering Quaker, Christian, social and international studies, and welcomes students, whether Friends or not, from this country and overseas. There are several adult education centres on Meeting House premises, such as those in Brighton and Plymouth, which run courses on a variety of subjects. Promoting thought about educational issues, both within and beyond the Society, is one of the functions of QSRE. This department also provides support for the Guild of Friends in Education.

Some Quaker institutions

Although in Friends' view education is a life-long process, their sphere of activity is largely concentrated among younger people. Quaker attention was directed to the needs of the elderly when, in the early days of the second world war, they became aware of the plight of many old people who wanted to leave their homes in danger areas, but had nowhere to go, nor anyone to care for them as their needs were not covered by official evacuation schemes. The Society responded by turning many of its country Meeting Houses into hostels until more suitable accommodation could be provided. The homes then established were staffed by members of the Friends Relief Service. Through this work Friends were made aware of the problems facing the elderly. At the close of the war some of these homes were retained by the Society, but many were passed over to local authorities. A variety of accommodation is now provided through some 29 housing associations. While Friends have a prior claim, residence is generally open to anyone.

The Bedford Institute Association based in Bunhill Fields

Meeting House in East London, exists to encourage new methods of dealing with inner city problems.

The Retreat, York, is a well-equipped mental hospital under Friends' auspices, where treatment is available for people suffering from mental illness. The Retreat was founded in 1796, as the outcome of the concern of a Quaker, William Tuke, a tea and coffee merchant, who was revolted by the appalling and sub-human attitude to mental illness then widely held. His hospital provided love and understanding, and this tradition has continued throughout the years.

There are seven guest houses under Quaker management which are open to the public, of these, Claridge House (Surrey) and Lattendales (Cumbria) are run by the Friends Fellowship of Healing especially welcoming people who need a quiet, restful atmosphere.

Friends and peace

From the beginning of Quakerism until the present time Friends have been convinced that as a religious society they must be concerned for peace, and do everything in their power to remove the scourge and threat of war from the world.

In 1661, at a time of great civil disturbance in this country, when the peaceable intentions of Friends had been questioned, a declaration was addressed to Charles II 'from the Harmless and Innocent People of God called Quakers', which said, 'We utterly deny all outward wars and strife and fightings with outward weapons, for any end, or under any pretence whatever; this is our testimony to the whole world . . .' This was a simple statement of the attitude of Friends themselves, but at the same time they also recognised that it was necessary to make constructive proposals to regulate relationships between nations. William Penn, one of the best known of the early Friends, in the founding of Pennsylvania, his 'holy experiment', and in such of his writings as *An Essay towards the Peace of Europe* (1693) well illustrates the practical and realist sides of the Quaker approach which complement the simple denial of 'all outward wars'.

Through three centuries Quakers have consistently followed this twofold approach to peace. In the mid-twentieth century, when peace-keeping and the issues of international relationships are infinitely more complicated than ever before, the Society still maintains its conviction that it is committed to building the institutions of peace.

In the words of the *Advices* Friends are urged to 'Be faithful in maintaining our witness against all war as inconsistent with the spirit and teaching of Christ. Seek, through his power and grace, to overcome in your own hearts the emotions which lie at the root of conflict'. Quakers also recognise that the causes of war are to be found in the structure of society and the Advice continues, 'In industrial strife, racial emnity and international tension, stand firmly by Christian principles, seeking to foster understanding between individuals, groups and nations'.

This corporately held witness of the Society sometimes strikes newcomers as impossibly idealistic. Yet as they have shared in Quaker worship and life they have discovered that it is not only possible but also the most sensible way to approach international affairs.

The problems of peacekeeping in the modern world are among the most intractable that mankind faces. To take but two examples, that of the Middle East and of Northern Ireland: clearly these are situations which certainly have no easy solution. In these and other areas Friends have been trying to make constructive proposals towards their resolution.

In such controversial situations it is not surprising that Friends are not always able to agree on the ways in which their concern for peace can be implemented. Some Friends would accept the idea of an international 'police' force, while others would reject this as a denial of their witness for peace, and would seek for a radical non-violent solution. The important thing in which all Quakers would unite is the recognition that peacemaking is an integral part of the Society's religious life.

Quakers in their witness for peace draw together a large number of varied strands. A considerable body of Friends share in peace vigils and marches, and have been active in such movements as CND. Others have studied the problems of disarmament and work for this cause. Many Friends have found their most constructive service through activities with the United Nations Association, the Fellowship of Reconciliation and other similar bodies.

An interesting development in recent years was the establishment of a University Chair of Peace Studies so that research could be made into the causes of conflict and ways of removing them. This concern began with an individual Friend and was ultimately shared by the whole Society. The outcome was that Bradford University allocated half the capital cost of setting up an academic department to undertake peace research, and the Society of Friends provided the other half by a public appeal. A Quaker was appointed as its first professor in 1973.

Quaker work for peace is focused in Quaker Peace & Service, which not only gives expert advice to the Society on all matters related to its concern, but also carries out an extensive programme of education and witness in and beyond Quaker circles. These activities include the sending of delegations where necessary to Ministers, Government Departments or Members of Parliament to discuss matters of policy. Arrangements are also made for groups of Friends to take part in missions of friendship abroad, and also in missions of fact finding and reconciliation to States in conflict.

William Penn House in London is a centre to which Quakers invite diplomats, politicians and experts in the field of international relations for general discussion and for consideration of particular issues. In many ways it is the counterpart of Quaker House, New York, which was established some years ago as a quiet place where representatives to the United Nations might meet informally with one another and with Friends. Such meetings have been warmly welcomed as opportunities where problems and difficulties can be shared with sympathetic and informed people. There are similar ventures in other parts of the world, notably Geneva and Delhi. Recently the Quaker Council for European Affairs established a Quaker House in Brussels 'to promote the traditions of the Society in the European context'.

Quakers, through the Friends World Committee for Consultation, have 'observer' status with the United Nations. During its General Assembly each autumn an international team of Friends augments the staff at Quaker House, New York, attends sessions of the Assembly, and has frequent meetings with delegates. In these ways Friends endeavour to give practical expression to their concern for peace, by supporting and encouraging diplomats and the staff of the United Nations who have to carry the heavy burden of peace-keeping. Much useful work is done among young diplomats from many countries through residential seminars in various parts of Europe, U.S.A., Japan and southern Asia. It is hoped that through free and uninhibited discussion of international affairs, those participating may gain real insight into the ways in which others look at the problems involved. Equally important are the personal friendships that are made. For in later years these people will become the diplomatic representatives of their nations.

Work camps

Just as important in Friends' eyes as gatherings of young diplomats, are Quaker work camps. These bring together international groups of people to carry through practical projects of various kinds, which, apart from this voluntary help, would not be done. These camps are yet another expression of the Quaker concern for peace building, as they do much to break down national and racial prejudice. International work camps demand considerable organisation, which is run by an office in Friends House.

Social responsibility

Some of the questions the Society addresses to its members ask, 'Are you working towards the removal of social injustices? Have you attempted to examine their causes objectively, and are you ready to abandon old prejudices and think again? Do you, as disciples of Christ, take a living interest in the social conditions of the district in which you live? Do you seek to promote the welfare of those in any kind of need, and a just distribution of the resources of the world?'

Quakers have a long tradition of work against slavery, and are still concerned about those areas of the world where slavery still continues. But in the main their attention nowadays has switched to the growing problem of race prejudice in this country. The Quaker Queries ask Friends, 'Do you behave with brotherly love to all men whatever their race, background or opinion? Do you try to make the stranger feel at home among you?'

In recent years the Society has recognised that it is increasingly difficult to deal with particular issues in isolation. Quaker Social Responsibility and Education seeks to coordinate the Quaker concern for race relations with the general concern for social and economic affairs. The Department has groups working on Addiction, Community Relations, Conservation and Environment, Industry and Work, Care for the Elderly, Penal Affairs and as mentioned earlier the Department cares for the Quaker concern for education.

Church unity

In much of the corporate work of the Society, Friends have been delighted to co-operate with their fellow Christians who are interested in similar spheres of service. As I have already mentioned a number of Meetings are represented on local councils of churches. The Society itself is an Associate Member of the British Council of Churches, and appoints two representatives. Friends also serve on its various departments, notably that concerned with international affairs, and on the British Churches Housing Trust.

A recent survey of the attitude of Monthly Meetings to church unity indicates a clear feeling that the separate entity of the Society of Friends should be preserved, but that co-operation with other branches of the Christian church should be continued and extended.

Young Friends

Young Friends maintain and organise their own activities. These include the arranging of national and international conferences, and the editing and publication of an exciting monthly journal *Young Quaker*. In many local areas flourishing Young Friends groups meet regularly.

Quakers overseas

Through Quaker Peace & Service, British and Irish Quakers are working in nearly a score of countries. In some instances the work is done side by side with American or Canadian Friends; in most, it is shared with the people of the country concerned: Indians, Pakistanis, Africans, Europeans, etc. Many of these local people eventually come to England for training with Quaker support and encouragement. In London an International Centre provides short term residence for people from abroad, especially students, and a meeting place for all nationalities.

This co-operation with people of other countries is an integral part of the Quaker faith. It springs from a belief that we need our neighbours and they need us, and each has something to learn from the other.

Overseas work depends first and last upon the existence of

some seventy or eighty people—teachers, social workers, agriculturalists, etc—who care for people and are anxious to minister to them by helping them to help themselves. The caring is of first importance, but it needs to be backed by faith and knowledge and skill. In this spirit many individual Friends have felt a personal concern to gain experience of other countries, especially the underdeveloped ones, and to make a small contribution to them by taking jobs abroad for a year or so.

In these ways Friends can express their traditional concern to relieve suffering, unconditionally and without partiality, in countries overseas. All Quaker work has its roots in our concern for our neighbour, and a conviction that love of neighbour and love of God are inseparably linked.

The Society is spread around the world, with groups of various sizes in Africa, Asia, Australasia, Europe and South and Central America, but by far the largest number is to be found in the United States. While the pattern of Quakerism followed by some sections of American Friends is similar to that described in this book, there are considerable groups that use a programmed form of worship, and appoint pastors to provide leadership. This pattern is also to be found in the large Friends group in East Africa.

In this century great strides have been made towards closer co-operation and unity among Friends through the holding of four world conferences, the second of which in 1937 led to the setting up of the Friends World Committee for Consultation.

Who pays?

Readers may well be wondering how Quakers finance the work that has been described, as well as the ordinary day to day costs of the Society. The running expenses of each Meeting are relatively low—after all there are no clergy or organists to pay—and costs are met by the gifts of people associated with them. Money is also required to maintain Meeting Houses, and when necessary to build new ones. This responsibility is usually carried by Monthly Meetings, sometimes in association with others. Loans and grants are available for these purposes from central funds.

A few large Monthly Meetings have full or part time secretaries, and a growing number of local Meetings appoint Wardens or Resident Friends. The Society itself employs some Friends to assist in the administration of its work. These include the Recording Clerk (the Society's General Secretary), a Finance Secretary and a Librarian. These Friends, and their small staff, are based in the headquarters of the Society at Friends House, Euston Road, London, NW1 2BJ. Also there are the secretaries and office staffs of the three departments. A total of about 100 people work in Friends House.

Finance and administration

The maintenance of the building in Euston Road is offset by the letting of rooms as offices, and for conferences and meetings. In fact such rents, together with interest on invested funds, provide a useful contribution to Quaker revenue. Each year an estimate is made of the amount of money required to run the Society, and this estimate is divided among Monthly Meetings according to the size of their membership. To this figure Monthly Meetings will add what they estimate they need for their purposes, and then ask Friends in their area to raise it. Usually a schedule is sent to each member (a family counts as one) indicating how much money is needed. The schedule also lists the three departments, schools, and other institutions or causes which do not receive direct support from the Society's budget.

Friends are free to decide which items they wish to support, and how much they feel they can afford to give. The amount will obviously vary according to their circumstances at different times of their lives. In my experience the Society's approach to its finances appeals to Friends as sensible, and when they are convinced that something is worth doing, there is never any difficulty in finding the money required. This is largely due to the fact that overhead expenses are deliberately kept to a minimum, and the knowledge that money subscribed will be carefully used. For this reason 'service' bodies like Quaker Peace & Service receive considerable financial support from outside the Society, including quite a lot of legacies. Quaker schools can usually count on the loyal support of old scholars, both Friends and non-Friends.

No hard and fast pattern can be laid down for the actual way in which a Friend will contribute. Some send one donation annually to the Monthly Meeting treasurer who allocates it according to their wishes. Some take out deeds of covenant, and many make periodic contributions either to the treasurer of their local Meeting or to a collection when they attend on Sunday. In most Meeting Houses there is an unobtrusive box near the door, and regular collections are made for different aspects of Quaker work, or other charities each week.

8

CAN I BECOME A QUAKER?

This book opened with a paragraph on the peculiar and confusing ideas many people have about Quakers; I hope what I have written will at least have dispelled some of them. I have already mentioned the widespread popular view that Quaker Meetings are private gatherings for members only, and that to be a Quaker you have to be born one. I propose to conclude my essay by saying something of what Friends do to make themselves known as a Society, and then to answer the question many people ask, 'Can I become a Quaker and, if so, how do I go about it?'

Making the Society known

Far from being in any way a closed shop, the Society warmly welcomes new people who are broadly in sympathy with Quaker attitudes to religion and life. Each Meeting will do all it can to make its own existence known, and to help people in the neighbourhood to find out about Quakers, and also to make them feel at home when they turn up at the Meeting House. But many people are naturally rather shy about getting in touch with a group of people whose popular image has probably scared them off. Also a local Meeting rarely has the resources to engage in intensive publicity, much of which in any case needs to be done centrally. The Society has therefore charged Quaker Home Service with the job of telling the public that Quakers exist, what they believe and are like, and of assuring them that they will be welcomed at their nearest Meeting House. The Department also has a general responsibility for encouraging the deepening of the spiritual life of the Society, and a special concern for Quaker children and young teenagers. In fulfilment of these tasks, books, pamphlets and a monthly magazine (see page 74) are published. Speakers are provided for meetings, both domestic and public.

For many years Quakers have used press advertisements to provide a little information about the Society, in the hope that it will arouse the interest of some people, who will then want to discover more. The emphasis in Quaker advertisements is strongly on information and facts: they are not devices aimed at persuading people to join the Society. Quakers have never been anxious to obtain new members merely for the sake of swelling their numbers, and the membership of London Yearly Meeting is only about 19,000, although between 300 to 400 people come into membership each year. Quakers have a deep dislike of proselytism, and have been criticised in some quarters for their lack of evangelical zeal. Many people who have realised that they are natural Quakers have often been extremely annoyed with the Society for apparently making it difficult for them to discover Friends. There is, I think, some truth in this criticism, and I would like to see much more done to make the Society known.

In response to advertising and information activities by Friends, in the press, on the radio and television, and through the display of posters, a considerable number of enquiries are received each year. To every person who responds, Quaker literature is sent together with the place and time of the nearest Meeting. No names are ever sent to local Friends, unless a specific request to be put in touch with them is received.

Enquirers

People who write (Quakers call them 'enquirers') react very differently to the literature and invitation they receive. Some ignore it altogether! Some go at once to their local Meeting take to it like a duck to water, and continue to attend regularly Quakers call these people 'attenders'. Others want to do a lot of thinking about Quaker ideas about religion before they take action by going to a Meeting. Even then they want to feel free to take their time in making up their minds, and naturally Quakers respect their reticence. Quite a lot of enquirers write for further information, and many ask particular questions on all kinds of issues, which the Quaker Home Service staff try to answer. Many have grave personal problems, and welcome the opportunity to seek confidential help: this is always gladly given, whether or not they are likely to become Friends. Some people engage in a long correspondence, or ask to be introduced to individual Friends, before they pluck up courage to attend a Meeting.

In recent years informal day and weekend conferences have been arranged to give enquirers the chance of discovering what they want to know about Quakerism, and also of actually meeting a few Friends. These have been warmly welcomed, and enquirers who have attended them discover to their delight the friendliness of Friends, and that their fears about Quaker quirks were ill-founded. As a result they have speedily sought out their home Meeting. Quaker Home Service will gladly send details of the times and places of Meetings, and also of enquirers' conferences, to anyone who asks.

From attender to member

Having passed from the stage of enquiring about the Society, to that of going to Meeting for Worship with some regularity, and therefore becoming acquainted with some members of the Meeting, most 'attenders' are likely to wonder whether they too might become members.

Because Quakers dislike thrusting their views on others, or bringing pressure upon them to become Friends, they have been extremely cautious about inviting attenders to consider whether they might apply for membership. In so far as this caution springs from a respect for people's freedom, and the desire to allow them time to make up their own minds, it is praiseworthy. Many attenders have welcomed the fact that Friends accept them as they are, and have not subjected them to demands to commit themselves before they are ready. Unfortunately, some attenders have interpreted this Quaker reticence as evidence that they are not wanted as members, and accordingly have not asked for membership because 'no one invited me to join'. Friends nowadays are slowly getting this message, and seek to encourage attenders by indicating how happy they would be if they applied for membership. However, the final initiative is still with the attender.

It is difficult to say exactly how attenders will know when the time has come for them to seek membership. For some this may be relatively soon after they have been sharing regularly in Quaker worship; for others the time may be much longer. As a rough guide I would feel that when attenders are reasonably sure that Meeting for Worship has become a necessary part of their lives, and when they find themselves at home in the company of Friends, and have a broad sympathy with their outlook, although complete agreement on every point is not required, then they should seriously consider applying for membership. Elders or overseers or any member of the Meeting with which they are associated will be very ready to talk over the position with them. In fact, it is always a good idea to seek such an informal conversation, in which particular questions can be answered, and the attenders helped to sort out any problems that inhibit their closer association with the Society.

Some people hesitate to seek membership because they feel that they do not match up to the high ideals of Quakerism. I do not know any members who feel that they do: if perfection were demanded, membership would rapidly dissolve! The important thing is the direction in which one is looking, and not the position one has reached. I have already made clear the fact that the Society happily contains a wide variety of religious outlook.

If for any reason attenders feel diffident in the first place, about approaching local Friends, they are very welcome to write to Quaker Home Service. Reading, too, can be a valuable introduction to Quaker thought and practice. Most Meeting Houses have some books available, and any local Friend or Quaker Home Service will be glad to recommend the books* likely to be most helpful. It is often a good idea for attenders to gain experience of Meetings other than their own if this is possible. In this way they will obtain a broader picture of Quaker life which will help them to understand more clearly how they feel about the Society.

Applying for membership

The actual procedure of applying for membership is quite simple. Attenders write a letter to the Clerk of the Monthly Meeting that covers the area of the Meeting they attend. The letter need contain no more than a simple request that they should be admitted into membership. It is however generally helpful if they say a little about themselves, and the reasons that have prompted the desire to become a Friend. As Friends wish an individual's link with the Society to be a truly personal one, the Monthly Meeting will arrange for two Friends, one of whom will usually know the applicant, to visit, so that in a personal meeting a real relationship may be established. In a friendly and informal atmosphere they can talk together and explore the reasons that have prompted the application and discuss the experience of Quaker life and worship. Questions can be asked and answered, and a description given of various aspects of Quakerism that are relevant. Put briefly, the people concerned seek to enter into a relationship with one another which will help to indicate whether or not the applicant is likely to be at home in the Society. Unfortunately, there is a wide popular belief among enquirers that the visit is a sort of inquisition, in which the enquirer is subjected to scrutiny under the Quaker microscope. I cannot emphasise too strongly that this not correct.

---

* A reading list will be found at the end of this book.

The Friends are acting as the representatives of their Monthly Meeting, and it is their job to help that Meeting to share in the relationship which the applicant has already established through attending a Quaker Meeting. This relationship will be furthered by the visitors' conversation. It is the recognition of the reality of the relationship between the applicant and the Society of Friends that constitutes the basis of membership. To help Friends achieve this, the visitors will tell the Monthly Meeting of the talk they have had with the applicant in a brief written report. They will, of course, respect anything that has been told to them in confidence. In most instances, after consideration of the report, the Monthly Meeting will record in a minute its acceptance into membership of the applicant. A Friend is usually asked to convey the Meeting's decision to newly admitted Friends, and to welcome them into membership.

Sometimes it will become apparent that the applicants should allow more time in which to become better acquainted with the Society, and in that case they will be advised to defer their applications for a period. It is also open to the Monthly Meeting to refuse membership to an applicant, but this rarely happens, as attenders will usually have talked over their position with members of their Meeting and have been sensitive about their advice about the suitability of making application for membership.

The minimum age for joining the Society is sixteen. Parents of younger children may obtain membership for them by making application to Monthly Meeting. Quite a number of parents do this, but others arrange for them to be listed as attenders, so that they may decide about membership themselves when they are old enough to join. Quakers do not use baptism, infant or adult, as a way to membership.

Why membership?

Membership makes no difference to the freedom of a person to attend Meeting for Worship. As I hope I have made abundantly clear, earlier, an attender, or even a passing visitor, is accepted as an integral part of the Meeting: there is no period of the Meeting that is reserved for members only, or particularly deep Meetings for Worship to which only Quakers are admitted. Why then bother with membership?

There are Friends who would like to see formal membership abolished, and others who would grant membership automatically to anyone who attended Meeting regularly. While I must confess to considerable sympathy with these views, I still feel that membership has value, for the needs both of the individual and of the Society. All these attitudes have been widely canvassed before the last revision of the regulations. Yearly Meeting 1966, after taking into account all the pros and cons of the various viewpoints, decided to retain membership.

Personal involvement

As I have indicated, membership of the Society is not a mere formality, but is the outward sign of a truly personal involvement with a group of people who share common convictions about the meaning and purpose of life. These arise from the still centre of their being and in their sense of identity with others when they are open to them in loving relationships. Their perception of the all-pervading value of love is deepened as they participate in the particular life of the Quaker community and share in its worship. There involvement in this turns them out again to the wider community.

For Quakers these experiences illuminate the meaning of the simple New Testament statement that 'God is love'. They know that they cannot be merely interested in religion—for religion is a way of life. Nor can they go this way alone, for they need the loving conern and care of their fellow Friends, in a community of people, where each one can count on the loyalty and support of others. In a body like the Society of Friends, which places such emphasis on personal relationships, it is natural that people committed to it will want to have that commitment recorded in membership. In saying this I am aware that there is a considerable number of attenders of many years standing, who in everything but name are Quakers, and certainly are accepted as such. I respect their hesitations that have caused them not to seek membership, although I must confess that I do not always understand them. I am, however, left with the feeling that both they and the Society would be enriched by their full commitment.

From the Society's point of view, it is useful and necessary to have a body of people on whom it may rely for support, and on whom, when necessary, it can rightly make demands for service. I can best illustrate this from my experience of my work at Friends House. From time to time I receive letters from people in distant parts of the country, who are not Friends, but feel that a religious Society with the name Friends can give them the personal help they require. From the way in which they write I realise that they need direct, personal assistance and friendship. In such circumstances I need to be able to turn to a Friend in their area, who is probably unknown to me, but whom I know I can trust and rely upon, because of a commitment marked through membership.

Membership is liable to affect your judgement in a Quaker business meeting. It is easier to commend a course of action, without fully weighing its long term results, when you are not finally responsible for it. But this is a somewhat negative point. The great thing about membership is that through it you can share in the life of the Society of Friends, enriching it by the contribution you have to make, and being enriched by its life.

Not such a bad lot

An introduction to the Quakers is one to a group of people whom I think you will find to be friendly, warm-hearted, humane and tolerant. While Quakers take life seriously they are not themselves impossibly serious, for they have tried to 'walk cheerfully over the world, answering that of God in everyone'.

Quakers, much to most people's surprise, have a nice sense of humour, and are even sometimes able to laugh at themselves. Through 300 years the Society has encouraged individuality in its members, which at the same time is successfully linked with a strong sense of community. This results in Quakers being on the whole interesting and lively people. It is many years since I myself joined the Society, and while there have been times when I have been hopping mad with Friends, as they have with me, I have never regretted the step I took.

As a result of this introduction to Quakers I hope that some of my readers will want to discover more about the Society of Friends. So let me introduce you to *Quaker Monthly*, a magazine specially produced with the needs of enquirers in mind. May I also remind you of the list of books and pamphlets for further reading on page 75.

Good though this material is, it cannot take the place of first-hand experience. This you can gain by going to a Quaker Meeting. You will be welcomed and no one will press you to go farther than you wish. So take your time and when you feel ready, follow Charles Lamb's advice and 'come with me into a Quaker's Meeting'.

9

SUGGESTIONS FOR FURTHER READING

General

Christian Faith and Practice in the Experience of the Society of Friends (London Yearly Meeting, 1960, *paper* £2.50, *hard* £3.50)

Church Government (London Yearly Meeting, 1968, rev. rpt. 1980, £2.50)

Advices and Queries (London Yearly Meeting, 1964, *card* 25 pence)

Quaker by Convincement by Geoffrey Hubbard (QHS, rev. rpt. 1985, £2.95)

Approach to Quakerism by Edgar Castle (QHS, 1961, rptd. 1979, £2.75)

The Discovery of Quakerism by Harold Loukes (QHS, 1960, rptd. 1981, £3.50)

Quakers in the Eighties: what it's like to be a Friend edited by Anne Hosking and Alison Sharman (QHS, 1980, reprinting)

Friends in the Americas by Francis B. Hall (Friends World Committee, 1976, £1.50)

George Fox

The Journal of George Fox edited by John Nickalls (London Yearly Meeting, 1952, rptd. 1975, *hard* £7, *paper* £4.50)

No more but my love: letters of George Fox selected and edited by Cecil W. Sharman (QHS, 1980, *hard* £4, *paper* £3)

Wait in the light: the spirituality of George Fox introductions by John Lampen (QHS, 1981, £2.75)

History

Portrait in Grey: a short history of the Quakers by John Punshon (QHS, 1984, rptd. 1986, £6.50)

The Beginnings of Quakerism by William C. Braithwaite (Sessions, 2nd edn., 1955, rptd. 1970, £9.50)

The Second period of Quakerism by William C. Braithwaite (Sessions, 2nd edn., 1961, £9.50)

The Later periods of Quakerism by Rufus Jones (Macmillan, 1921, out of print)

Worship, prayer and devotion

The Amazing fact of Quaker worship by George H. Gorman (QHS, 1973, rptd. 1979, £2.25)

An Exercise of the spirit: Quakers and prayer compiled by Leila Ward. Edited by Ruth W. Bell and Anne Hosking (QHS, 1984, £1.50)

Steps in a Large Room: a Quaker explores the monastic tradition by Christopher Holdsworth (QHS, 1985, £2.50)

The Desert and the Market Place by Jack Dobbs (QHS, 1984, 80 pence)

God is silence by Pierre Lacout (QHS, 1970, rptd. 1985, 80 pence)

Preparation for worship by Thomas Green (QHS, 1952, rptd. 1983, 80 pence)

'Where words come from.' An interpretation of the ground and practice of Quaker worship and ministry by Douglas Steere (QHS, 1955, rptd. 1985, £1.75)

A Testament of Devotion by Thomas Kelly (QHS, 1941, rptd. 1979, £2.50)

Bible

The Bible and the Light Within by George Boobyer (QHS, 1973, rptd. 1981, 80 pence)

The Spiritual Quest: some suggestions for Bible study by Meg Chignell (QHS, 1983, £2.50)

Twenty Questions about Jesus by John Lampen (QHS, 1985, £2.95)

Theology and doctrine

What canst thou say? Towards a Quaker theology by Janet Scott (QHS, 1980, reprinting)

Reasonable Uncertainty: a Quaker approach to doctrine by Gerald Priestland (QHS, 1982, £2)

Modern Quakers

The Christian Life—lived experimentally: an anthology of the writings of Kathleen Lonsdale selected by James Hough (QHS, 1976, rptd. 1980, £1.50)

Will Warren: a scrapbook. A Quaker in Northern Ireland compiled by John Lampen (QHS, 1983, £1.50)

The way out is the way in. A Quaker's pilgrimage by Damaris Parker-Rhodes (QHS, 1985, £3.95)

Search for reality in religion. Reflections on seeking the fellowship of the Society of Friends by John Macmurray (QHS, 1965, rptd. 1984, £1.25)

Quaker work and witness

Quaker encounters by J. Ormerod Greenwood (Sessions, 1975-8, 3 vols, *each* £7). A study of two centuries of Quaker activity in the relief of suffering caused by war or natural calamity

The Past is prologue: 100 years of Quaker overseas work 1868-1968 by Edward Milligan (QPS, 1968, 50 pence)

Prophets and Reconcilers: reflections on the Quaker Peace Testimony by Wolf Mendl (QHS, 1974, £1.50)

True Justice: Quaker peacemaking and peacemakers by Adam Curle (QHS, 1981, £2)

Social responsibility

Six Quakers look at crime and punishment (QHS/QSRE, 2nd edn., 1985, £1.60)

Facing Death by Diana Lampen (QHS, 1979, £2)

Turn a new leaf: six essays on work by Lorraine Brown *et al* (QHS/QSRE, 1983, £1.20)

There is a unity: Quaker thoughts on racial justice edited by Peggy Heeks and Martin Wyatt (QHS/QSRE, 1984, £1.20)

Towards a Quaker view of sex: an essay by a group of Friends (QHS, 2nd edn., 1964, rptd. 1979, 90 pence)

Children

A measure of our values: goals and dilemmas in the upbringing of children by Michael Rutter (QHS, 1983, £3)

For younger readers

You and the Quakers: a book about the Society of Friends for young people by Alison Sharman (QHS, 2nd edn., 1985, £1.75)

The Quakers by Hope Hay (Ward Lock, 1981, £1.50)

The Society of Friends by George Gorman (Religious Education Press, 1978, rptd. 1983, £1.90)

The Arts

Quakers and the arts: a survey of attitudes of British Friends to the creative arts from the 17th to the 20th century by Frederick Nicholson (QHS, 1968, £1.50)

All the books listed above are obtainable from the FRIENDS BOOK CENTRE, FRIENDS HOUSE, EUSTON ROAD, LONDON NW1 2BJ. This list is only a selection. A full catalogue of Quaker literature will be sent on request.

INDEX